5 Ways Teens Can Make Money This Summer

By

Stan Martin

Career Coach & Job Developer.

www.empowercareer.net & www.7dayjob.com

Disclaimer

The information presented in this report solely and fully represents the views of the author as of the date of publication. Any omission, or potential misrepresentation of, an peoples or companies is entirely unintentional. As a result of changing information, conditions or contexts, this author reserves the right to alter content at their sole discretion impunity.

The report is for informational purposes only and while every attempt has been made to verify the information contained herein, the author assumes no responsibility for errors, inaccuracies, and omissions. Each person has unique needs and this book cannot take these individual differences into account. For ease of use, all links in this report are redirected through this link to facilitate an future changes and minimize dead links.

This book is copyright © 2017 by "**Stan Martin Career Coach & Job Developer**" with all rights reserved. It is illegal to copy, distribute, or create derivative works from this ebook in whole or in part. No part of this report may be reproduced or transmitted in any form whatsoever, electronic, or mechanical, including photocopying, recording, or by an informational storage or retrieval system without expressed written, dated and signed permission from the author.

TABLE OF CONTENTS

Completing Surveys Online 4

Washing Cars 5

Dogsitting 7

Blogging 9

Sell Online Or Offline 11

Other Means through which Teens Can Make Money 13

Bonus Opportunities 15

Connect with us 16

3 Careers You Can Make Over 60k Without A Degree 17

COMPLETING SURVEYS ONLINE

The new way through which teens can make money is by giving their opinion filling out surveys online. This is a job that they can do from home and, you can pick the hours. No worries about working late before a big test in school or not having the time to get homework done.

Completing surveys is a legitimate way teens can make money. Thousands of adults are making money by completing surveys online, and teens can do it too. In fact, teens are needed because their opinions are required. If a product is about to be launched that is geared toward teenagers, who better to give their opinion about it than teens.

Payment for completing surveys can be in a variety of forms. For most, the best is cash. Surveys can pay anywhere from $5 to $75 depending on the survey. Some surveys are product reviews, you are sent the product, and after reviewing it, you get to keep the product. That can be a good way to get some fun things around the house. Other surveys pay by submitting your name in a drawing for prizes or cash.

You can find the survey companies online. Big companies pay market research companies to get opinions on their products. The research companies create surveys and the criteria for who should complete them. The survey company goes to their list of participants and sends out survey invitations to those who have expressed interest in completing surveys and meet the qualifications. You have the option to complete the survey or wait for another. To keep a good flow of surveys invitations coming, you should sign up with at least 150 companies

WASHING CARS

Resourceful teens and kids are forever searching for ways to make a few extra dollars for that next CD or tank of gas for their car. For the industrious kid wanting to make some serious cash, detailing cars can become a serious business.

People are on the go these days and never in our history have we been busier. The result of all that running around is that either many chores get left undone or more likely people look for others to do some of those chores for them. Whether it is house cleaning, lawn maintenance or detailing cars, this leaves a wide open market for the neighborhood teens.

Car Detailing left to the professionals is an expensive proposition; a car wash can cost a person $20-$30 and a full detail will run them well over $100, or a car owner can find the time to do it themselves. With these options available to them, a busy car owner is often happy to find a willing teen to wash their car for them.

To get started, you will first need to decide what services you will offer, washing cars is the simplest, least expensive and perhaps will be the most popular, but you can make considerably more money by offering a few extras to your customers. Offer to wax their car, polish their wheels, vacuum carpets and clean the leather or vinyl. Make sure you do your research on how to clean these items properly, and how to select the best equipment and products to get the job done.

Call around to the various car detailing businesses to find out what they charge for their services, then severely undercut them. Be sure to take into account the cost of your supplies, travel costs, and the amount of labor you will put into a job as you figure your prices.

Once you have your services and prices decided on, it is time to advertise, and the best way to accomplish this is with fliers and business cards. Hang them on bulletin boards where ever you see them, many hardware stores, automotive stores, and most grocery stores have them.

Take your fliers door to door, and put them on every dirty car you see. Hand out business cards to the new and used car lots, times are tough right now and if they cannot afford professional detailing services they might be willing to let you wash their cars for them.

Car detailing has the potential to be a very profitable business for a teen, and it can be done with very little expenses and equipment, making it an ideal way to fill your empty wallet.

DOGSITTING

Are you a kid or teen who loves animals and wants to find a way to make some extra money? If you are good with dogs, and like the outdoors, you might have a winning combination.

These days people are very busy; often between working and commuting, they spend 10-12 hours or more a day, away from home. For many of these employees, this means owning a dog is out of the question, since dogs need lots of exercises, and let out to do their business on a regular basis. Sadly many of them would love to own a dog that would greet them at the door each day, and curl up next to them at night.

There is a solution for them and an opportunity for you, the animal loving kid, to make a bit of extra income. Dog walking and sitting services are becoming very popular these days, as an alternative way for busy professionals to have the option to own a dog, even when they cannot be home all the time.

One of the best ways to begin your new business is to get to know the dogs in your neighborhood and their owners. If it is OK with the owners, spend time playing with their dogs and develop a friendship with both dog and owner.

If the owners work a lot, offer to walk their dogs after you get home from school, or to play with them in the afternoons in their fenced in back yards. Be sure to choose dogs that you are certain you can handle, given your size and age; you do not want them getting away.

You can also put up fliers around your neighborhood and local stores, advertising what services you will offer, such as walking, feeding and watering, grooming, or playing with their dogs, and how to contact you. Older teens may also want to offer more advanced services for owners who need to go out of town or have special needs dogs, and this could include giving dogs their medication or caring for elderly or disabled dogs during the day.

Be sure you read up on walking and caring for dogs, consider their safety and yours, and be certain you know what to do if confronted with another dog. Read up on first aid for dogs, and be sure you have emergency numbers for the owner and vet should the worst happen and the dog needs medical care.

Walking and caring for dogs can be a very fulfilling and enjoyable way to make extra money, and depending on the area you live in you may find that you have your very own profitable business in no time.

BLOGGING

One of the greatest things to happen on the internet is blogs. As a teen, you like to share your experiences with others. Blogging is the best way to go about. Don't just start to include each and everything in your blog.

First, think of some topic which you are interested in. Then register for a free blog at blogger.com. Now slowly and steadily post articles on that blog. Spread it among your friends and also on the web. You can then add some ads, sell some products and also write some paid reviews. This way you will earn money by doing your favorite stuff.

Teens have many different interests that can be used to make a blog. Once a topic is picked to write about, there are several ways you can make money with it. The most obvious is to add banners and advertisements on the side of the blog. The affiliate link that is being promoted on Myspace or Facebook can also be promoted on the blog. AdSense is the most common ad company, but because there are so many AdSense ads, internet viewers' eyes have become trained just to pass over and ignore the ads. One good feature of AdSense is a search box that can be placed on the blog. The search is powered by Google and money earned for every search. This not only earns money but is convenient for the reader to find old posts. There are also programs similar to the review writing except that the review is posted on the blog rather than on the review site itself. The site assigns a review to the blogger and a fixed amount for every review. The downside is that the article most likely won't be relevant to the topic of the blog. Many bloggers call it a "sponsored review" which tells their readers that they are being paid to write the post. Blogging is only a good option for teens who want to seriously make money online because it requires so much work to get traffic and write blog posts often. However, once a readership is built up, blogging can be very profitable because of the money earned through affiliate links and advertisements. The upside to blogging, as opposed to Myspace, is that all the people looking at the blog are there is to see the content. If the advertisements are targeted than the people will see ads relevant to them. So a number of people who click on ads will be greater.

SELL ONLINE OR OFFLINE

In these days and time, we are living in an age of global business; the internet has provided a very versatile platform for all of us to create and run businesses. This does not leave the teens out either. In fact, it has even increased tremendously the ways teens make money given the fact that this group more readily accept and adopt new changes. The wealthiest teens out there are running their online businesses.

There are teens, however, who stick to their 'traditional sources' of income e.g. lawn mowing, working on stores, offering computer skills. While these sources are some of the sure ways teens can earn some money, it cannot make you much money as having your own business. Furthermore, these jobs require you to perform the work directly. This means that if you cannot perform the work yourself, you are not entitled to earn anything. Even though online business requires much labor and skills from your side, you can always outsource some duties. In most instances, automated systems are used.

The surest way for teens to make themselves rich online is to create and sell their products from their e-commerce website or blog. Unlike affiliate marketing where you only earn commission for what you sell, with your products you can make money through many ways and allow you to brand your name and business. There are several ways teens can create products. The widely applied are;

Creating the product yourself.

The most suitable products for teens to sell online are digital products since they can be created cheaply no storage or shipping cost. In some instances, you can distribute your products to other online stores to sell for you. These digital products can be software, e-books, online videos or audio. Ebooks are the easiest to create. If you already have the content, then you can compile your work into PDF format using free PDF conversion tools.

Outsourcing

For some of the teens who find, coming up with interesting information a daunting task, then they can hire experts at outsourcing sites. Although it requires some money, it is always the best way to create a product if you don't have the skills or time. Even the most successful online entrepreneurs today, do outsource their work. The best places to find experts are outsourcing sites e.g. guru.com, elance.com. On these sites, you will find ghostwriters, software programmers, marketers, and web designers ready to do the work.

Marketing your products online can be a challenge to many teens but if then can follow the right marketing strategy by starting with few traffic sources then expand to more expensive advertising. If you want to become a rich teen, then you should consider selling your own products through your own website. This will allow you to develop a sustainable online business

OTHER MEANS THROUGH WHICH TEENS CAN MAKE MONEY

Retail/Food Service

Many teens of working age (15 and up) find after school or weekend work at local fast food restaurants or in retail stores in the mall. Many such establishments will work with a teen on schedules and offer minimum wage.

Babysitter

With so many parents having to go back to work, there is a larger need for after school child care. Teens who are too young to work in retail can find work sitting with neighborhood children.

Handy Person

If you live in a community where there are elderly neighbors or single moms, a teen can find lots of odd jobs to do. Teens can do lawn care, painting, snow removal, and general repairs on a regular or as-needed basis. Go door to door or posts "work wanted" signs at the local grocery store.

Computer Lessons

For teens who are technologically advanced, they can earn some side money teaching others how to use computers and software. There are many adults who are not computer literate and would likely pay for lessons in basic knowledge of software and internet.

Paid Internships

Teens who have an idea of what they want to be "when they grow up" might be able to secure a paid internship in the industry they plan to pursue. This internship will not only earn them an income but it will also provide invaluable information and experience teens can carry with them after high school graduation. If you have friends or relatives in the industry of choice, ask for referrals on paid internship opportunities or speak with the school's guidance counselor.

Selling Skills

If a teen is artistically inclined, they can visit weekend farmer's markets or other locations and provide characters or drawings of customers. There are many skills a teen may have developed at a young age and can easily learn how to earn money using their skills. This can be their first lesson in freelancing towards a profitable future career.

Tutoring

If your teen excels at a particular subject, they can advertise their tutoring services around the community or throughout the school. Tutoring often generates a decent hourly pay, and if the teen can take on coaching work for more than one student at a time, they can earn a nice income.

All teens will have different ideas about how they want to earn money, and there are many opportunities available to them if they have the support and encouragement from their parents. Teens who learn money management lessons now will likely avoid debt hassles in the future.

BONUS OPPORTUNITIES

Arts and Crafts Production and Sales

There may be a market for items that you create, especially during the winter holidays.Towards the end of the year, schools and churches hold arts and crafts fairs, and eager shoppers line up to buy Christmas ornaments, wreaths, and last-minute gifts. Summer art festivals can also be an opportunity to sell art and handmade jewelry. Booth and table rental costs vary, but if you partner with a friend or a neighbor who also has items to sell, it won't cost as much and you can help each other out. Sales can be sporadic, and although the money can be considerable, it likely won't replace a steady income. In addition, you will have to pay for supplies, and pay rental fees for booth or table space at fairs and festivals. If you'd rather set up shop online, consider selling your arts and crafts on Etsy.

Document and Photograph Archival Services

Many people need documents and photos scanned, stored, and archived, but few people have the time to take on this considerable chore. My family has thousands of photos from the pre-digital camera era. They would love to have all of the photos scanned and safely stored online or saved to a computer file, but no one has the time to tackle this time-consuming task.

Start this part-time business by networking with your parents' friends to offer scanning, storage, and archival services for their documents and photos. Documents can be archived to Google Docs and photos can be scanned and stored on DVDs, websites, and computers. Agree on the number of photos or documents that need to be scanned or archived, and then set a price per item based on the length of time it will take to complete the tasks. Pricing for scanning and archival services will vary, but a range might include $0.25 per photo and $0.35 per document page. The work can be tedious, and you'll have to handle documents and photos carefully, to ensure they aren't damaged or lost.

CONNECT WITH US

You tube Channel: http://www.youtube.com/c/StanleyMartin74

Tumblr: http://empowercareer.tumblr.com

Facebook: https://www.facebook.com/empowercareer

Pinterest: http://www.pinterest.com/empowercareer

Twitter: https://twitter.com/7dayjob

Instagram: https://www.instagram.com/empower_career_coach/

LinkedIn: https://www.linkedin.com/in/stanmartin

Blog: www.empowercareer.net & www.7dayjob.com

3 CAREERS YOU CAN MAKE OVER 60K WITHOUT A DEGREE

You have finished high school and thinking of doing something productive. Agreeably, you cannot aim to be the top boss of a firm from day one itself. You will need to get a degree and study more and then start from a job and climb up the corporate ladder step-by-step. However, in the present days, there are career options paying you over 60k without a degree too. The secret to getting this rather decent paycheck is by knowing where to apply.

Make your CV and start applying across diverse companies. Be open to learning and knowing and that is the first big step to success.

Pre-requisite Traits to Possess Before You Apply

Eagerness: How eager are you to start working is what makes you go ahead and make the big cut!
Kick out Laziness: If you are lethargic, you might find it very difficult from day one.
Never Say Die Attitude: Failure to crack every interview just means you are trying.
Know People Better: Be ready to discover your real personality as you meet new people.
Knowledge: You get to learn from every single day at work. Learn and evolve!
Let us now discuss the top three career choices you can make and draw 60k without a degree.

Air Traffic Controllers
The position requires you to manage the air traffic with great caution. Once you join, you are required to pass the tests by the FAA, which also includes a battery of mental and medical checks. The maximum age for taking this test is 31. Your work will include directing the air traffic and

manage the takeoff, landing, and even the emergency landings with great precision.

IT Manager / Networking

Companies usually hire IT guys to ensure their servers and computers work smoothly. You need to possess certification in Networking to have the technical know-how and that's about it. You can look for jobs in companies like HP, Microsoft, Oracle, and other such IT firms. The pay can reach up to $125,101.

Financial Consultants

If you love to observe the finance market and have a knack of consulting, working as a consultant will be a great career option for you. Just a high school education and an aptitude to help clients get the best finances for their businesses or personal use will be your work. You can specialize and seek employment in the firms like KPMG, Ernst and Young and others with a reasonably good pay package.

Other Career Options to Consider

There are scores of moneymaking options in the market and some even in technical fields. There are offbeat options like an entrepreneur of a startup venture, or a court report, a real estate agent, an executive chef and many more. The only thing you need to focus on while taking up these jobs is to know your passion. Unless you are passionate about the career choice, it can never be your identity for long.

5 WAYS TEENS CAN MAKE MONEY THIS SUMMER

LOOKING FOR A JOB?

- Search for Great Jobs & Careers
- Search for Work at Home Jobs
- Search for High paying jobs
- Search for side jobs
- Search for Jobs with Amazon, Home Depot, Walmart, and other Fortune 500 companies
- Find great tips and articles on our career blog
- Sign up for Free Job Alerts
- Post your resume and start today!

VISIT WWW.EMPOWERCAREER.NET
FIND GREAT CAREER OPPORTUNITIES

COMPANIES ARE HIRING NOW!
DISCOVER THE HIDDEN JOB MARKET! FIND OUT WHERE ALL THE JOBS ARE!
JOBS AND CAREERS IN THE UNITED STATES AND ACROSS THE WORLD

WWW.EMPOWERCAREER.NET

Employers post your job openings on Job Finder. To post your job or for more info please visit www.empowercareer.net or email smartin@empowercareer.net

JobFinder

Empower Career

© 2017 Stan Martin Career Coach & Job Developer
www.empowercareer.net & www.7dayjob.com

5 WAYS TEENS CAN MAKE MONEY THIS SUMMER

www.7dayjob.com

Amazon Virtual Jobs- Work from Home

Work from Home

Click Here

5 WAYS TEENS CAN MAKE MONEY THIS SUMMER

www.ingramcontent.com/pod-product-compliance
Lightning Source LLC
Chambersburg PA
CBHW020716180526
45163CB00008B/3108